BRITAIN IN OLD PHOTOGRAPHS

# SEDGLEY & DISTRICT
## A THIRD SELECTION

TREVOR GENGE

SUTTON PUBLISHING LIMITED

Sutton Publishing Limited
Phoenix Mill · Thrupp · Stroud
Gloucestershire · GL5 2BU

First published 1999

*Title page photograph*: Children gather
around the saplings on the Birmingham
New Road, 1927. The trees commemorated
Coseley's First World War dead.

**British Library Cataloguing in Publication Data**
A catalogue record for this book is available from the
British Library.

ISBN 0-7509-2215-X

Typeset in 10½/13½ Photina.
Typesetting and origination by
Sutton Publishing Limited.
Printed in Great Britain by
Ebenezer Baylis, Worcester.

# THE BLACK COUNTRY SOCIETY

This voluntary society, affiliated to the Civic Trust, was founded
in 1967 as a reaction to the trend of the late 1950s and early 1960s
to amalgamate everything into large units and in the Midlands to
sweep away the area's industrial heritage in the process.

The general aim of the Society is to create interest in the past, present and future of
the Black Country, and early on it campaigned for the establishment of an industrial
museum. In 1975 the Black Country Museum was started by Dudley Borough Council
on 26 acres of totally derelict land adjoining the grounds of Dudley Castle. This has
developed into an award-winning museum which attracts over 250,000 visitors annually.

At the Black Country Museum there is a boat dock fully equipped to restore narrow
boats of wood and iron and different boats can be seen on the dock throughout the year.
From behind the Bottle and Glass Inn visitors can travel on a canal boat into Dudley
Canal Tunnel, a memorable journey to see spectacular limestone caverns and the
fascinating Castle Mill Basin.

There are over two thousand members of the Black Country Society and all receive
the quarterly magazine *The Blackcountryman*, of which over 119 issues have been
published since its founding in 1967. In the whole collection there are some 1,700
authoritative articles on all aspects of the Black Country by historians, teachers,
researchers, students, subject experts and ordinary folk with an extraordinary story to tell.
The whole constitutes a unique resource about the area and is a mine of information for
students and researchers who frequently refer to it. Many schools and libraries are
subscribers. Three thousand copies of the magazine are printed each quarter. It is non-
commercial, and contributors do not receive payment for their articles.

*PO Box 71 · Kingswinford · West Midlands DY6 9YN*

# CONTENTS

Traffic around Sedgley Bull Ring, 1967.

The ceramic mural, by local artist William H. Burgess, for Sedgley Local History Museum, Brick Street. The mural portrays both features and people who influenced the manor's history. It hangs over the internal entrance to the museum, situated within the Old Nail Warehouse renovated and used by Cottage Blinds.

# INTRODUCTION

Can there possibly be more photographs of the Sedgley area that we have not seen? A valid question, and one asked each time a further selection is undertaken. I never cease to be astonished by the people who either acquaint me with new material, or possess it themselves, and are willing to share it with others through the pages of these books. In addition I am appreciative of those who present me with the challenge to remedy omissions from previous books, or point me towards better photographs.

This third selection draws on established archives but, as always, benefits from those who have retained, in album and cupboard, photographic evidence of scenes and moments important to their locality or families past, and also have the understanding to recognise its timeless value to others. Once more we are able to enter the places dear to our own memory or even those only spoken of by our ancestors.

The first two volumes of *Sedgley & District in Old Photographs* have already presented the ancient Manor of Sedgley, its former boundaries and distinctive village and hamlet centres, and attempted to tell a story that is demonstrably twelve or thirteen hundred years old. In addition the area was undoubtedly crossed by the Romans and has a known prehistoric Stone Age site. The limestone ridge of Sedgley Beacon through Wrens Nest to Castle Hill yields fossils from the ancient sea bed that are some 400 million years old.

Photographic evidence is limited to the last two centuries, of course, while improvements in cameras and development and printing techniques tends to lead towards a predominance of photographs from the twentieth century. For all this, the oldest photograph yet included in the Sedgley series appears in this volume. This is a photograph taken in the vicarage garden of Christ Church, Coseley, which had almost the appearance of 'tea stains' until computer restored. Grainy it may be, but its date of 1868 makes it a remarkable witness to that moment.

In this selection we shall be reminded again of how influenced we were by both industry and agriculture in our 'black' and 'green' country. Once more we shall be made aware of lost buildings, some architectural treasures and others plain, but holding particular memories of people, and times. Perhaps, too, it will help us to decide to protect the buildings we still have. We are a world away from the destructive 1970s. Thankfully, today the word more frequently used is preservation, even when structural alterations are required.

In this book's pages we may look again at old streets and the shops that served them. Of these some may best be remembered in folk museums, but we shall not often see the community spirit that existed within them unless we value it enough to want to recreate it. Those teeming communities so often met and socialised close to home, before supermarkets, shopping malls and easy transport changed our lifestyles.

The extensive population growth brought about by the Industrial Revolution changed the face of the manor, and also its local government. The old Sedgley Board covered the entire manor, its poor, its health, its law and order – and as the population grew it became practically unworkable. The first change came from the creation of two boards, Upper Sedgley and Lower Sedgley, and officers were appointed to administer the two areas separately. This was a long process that was finally completed in 1867.

Similar problems arose in other parts of the country too, and national government introduced a succession of local government acts. Thus in 1894–5 Sedgley and Coseley attained independent urban district status, and the ancient manor of Sedgley was effectively divided.

At first schools were not within the urban district's control, as so many of them were church schools, but the growth of board schools, occasioned by the 1870s Act, slowly changed the balance and meant that some of the church schools were not replaced. The council schools were so described from 1902 onwards.

In the long history of our area this fundamental change, to urban districts, is seen to have been short lived, for just seventy years later new metropolitan boroughs encompassed almost the whole area. Today Dudley, Wolverhampton and Walsall Metropolitan Boroughs, and also South Staffordshire, share the lands once known as Sedgley. These photographs, in the main, cover the time before this last development took place, and give us an opportunity to consider those earlier days.

There is a world of community life to reconsider and to value, of public service, of church and chapel, of school, local shopkeeper and pub. There is the impact of the canal, railway, motor vehicle, the delivery van, the charabanc and the coach. The world of recreation and sport has also played its part. All of this has in many ways enriched the lives of Sedgley's inhabitants, and provides the substance of their memories. But above all, as the photographs are seen, I am sure that it will be the people who lived in Sedgley that will provide our richest memories.

As the writer, I am increasingly conscious of the indebtedness one has to those who have provided illustrations and information, known perhaps only to themselves, that make these books a source of discussion and often provokes further information – which in turn contributes to the recorded memory (or history) of our manor.

# CHAPTER ONE

# STREETS, ROADS & LANES

*An ancient footpath (a bier way) from Gospel End and*
*Sedgley Hall to All Saints' Parish Church. It could be*
*a thousand years old.*

Parkes Hall Road still had these old stone cottages, some still with shutters, in the late 1950s.

Brook Street, Woodsetton, contained this cottage row in 1959. They appear to have been braced together against subsidence.

In 1958 Anchor Lane had an entrance from the Birmingham New Road. This was subsequently removed at the road's upgrading. It led to the Anchor Inn (see page 84) and the little community surrounding it (see book 2). Now it is part of a small industrial estate, and houses a Wolverhampton waste disposal amenity site.

The lane as it neared the Anchor canal bridge, and the inn. It passed on to join Anchor Road. These buildings have since been demolished.

The most ancient of Sedgley's paths is the ridge path along the Beacon. This view, looking south towards the Monument Tower (see book 2) and the water tanks, shows that constant erosion has revealed the limestone of the hill.

The same path, looking north, as it descends towards the plateau, was aptly named 'Breakheart Hill'. The land to the east was ploughed right to the ridge path, and must have presented a challenge to the horses and ploughmen as they climbed from the bottom. It was to justify its name further when tragically, in the 1940s, it was the scene of a murder.

Boys play in the road to Fellows' Farm (see book 2),
1959. The old road remains as a footpath between
Tipton Road and Marlborough Road.

This 'road,' seen here in 1959, was known as the
'Rough Road'. It provided an alternative way to
Fellows' Farm, passing stone cottages on its way. The
cottages had no piped water. The entrance to the road
is the footpath on the west side of High Arcal Drive,
along which pupils from High Arcal G.M. secondary
school now make their way to school.

This wonderful view of Sedgley High Street and Bull Ring, without its traffic island, can only have been taken from the top of the tram, *c.* 1910. It presents a leisurely view of a sunny evening in the village centre. Danger from traffic is small. The large house (left) was originally a farmhouse. The tram route, along Dudley Street, leaves the Bull Ring sharply to the left, while the older road direction, along Dean Street, is clearly visible.

Jevon Street, Roseville, Coseley, 1960. Jevon Street is climbing the hill ahead, while Castle Street leads off to the left. Castle Street became the main shopping street off the older centre of the community, The Square. The shops on the corner are Davies' cakes and bread shop and Fellows' hardware stores. The name Jevon relates to an old local family who had lived in Sedgley from early in the seventeenth century at Sedgley Hall. Further branches of the family lived in the Gornals and at Tipton.

Castle Street, Roseville, Coseley, takes its name from the very visible castle (see book 1). Views of the castle are also claimed by several local houses. Here in the late 1960s, looking south, Udall & Sons butcher's is separated from the chemist's by Udall's yard. A wide variety of shops followed, studded by a number of public houses.

Castle Street, looking north, showing that some of the houses have survived the change to shops, and also what the old, early Victorian Street might have looked like.

A glimpse of old Bayer Street, Coseley. Legend has it that the name is more properly Bear Street, in honour of The Bear public house that stood within it, while local dialect did the rest. Note the scrubbed, and sometimes whitened, steps.

The east end of School Street, 1962, demolished about six years later. The pram, parked unattended (one hopes without an occupant), and the wide open front door speak of a sense of security no longer enjoyed.

Old Green Street, Roseville, Coseley, May 1967. Modern Green Street is now wider and longer, and a by-pass to ensure speedier passage for traffic through Roseville, greatly reducing traffic through Castle Street. It does not follow the exact line of old Green Street, though happily retains the name. This picture shows the street as it heads towards Canal Street. Its houses are typical Victorian terrace, with a shared entry.

Old School Street, 1967. The building on the distant right-hand corner is the Council House, in Green Street. The school is the Wesleyan Sunday school, and can be seen on the left beyond Green Street, which then ended at School Street.

Turner Street, Lower Gornal, 1970s. St James Street is on the right and Turner Street descends towards Humphrey Street. The hills beyond are of the old area known as Graveyard.

This sunny view is St James' Street looking towards Turner Street. The street takes its name from St James' Church, and shows that, in 1970, little had changed in the character of these Lower Gornal streets.

Abbey Street in Gornal Wood, Lower Gornal, shows the typical, mid-Victorian design of houses with front doors straight on to the pavement, and without the tiny 'token' front gardens that appeared mostly after 1875. In this 1960s' view the communal entry has been bricked up.

This 'back entry' in North Street, Lower Gornal, is in use during the 1970s.

Zoar Street descends to the natural square graced by the Methodist church of that name (see book 2). Photographed in the 1970s, it is part of a long descending lane from the ridge, through Lower Gornal into Gornal Wood. Red Hall Junior School is on the left and the Infant School to the right.

Dibdale Street, Lower Gornal, 1960s. Dibdale Street runs south from Dibdale Road, into a valley. At the bottom it leaves Sedgley and enters Dudley. Old Russell's Hall was near this boundary. Modern houses now mark the entrance to the street. A factory still occupies the site on the right.

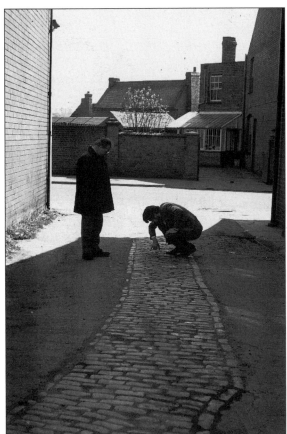

Louise Street, Gornal Wood, Lower Gornal, 1970s. Interest is being shown in an old foot or truck way made from cobbles.

The rear of Price's Row and Prospect Place, Gornal Wood, 1960s. The gable end in the foreground is built from the local Gornal stone.

Bridge Street, *c.* 1950. An interesting junction of streets lay at the edge of old Wallbrook, in Coseley. The photograph shows the entrance to White Street, immediately right. Bayer Street is crossing the railway bridge to the left, and before the bridge the strangely but appropriately named Angle Street bends right.

Approaching The Square, Roseville, Coseley, from Avenue Road, 1962. Roseville House is on the left, in Bayer Street, and the yard and inn sign, beyond the roundabout, indicate The Chainyard, a clear reference to an old Coseley trade.

Bridge Street, Wallbrook, Coseley, 1950s. The photograph shows an interesting mixture of building styles, outhouses and large yard gates. An exposed wall is painted with gas tar to resist damp.

Looking back down Bridge Street we see the corner shop and dwelling, and another shop serving its local community.

Earlier nineteenth-century houses on the corner of Chapel Street and Bridge Street, Wallbrook, 1946. None of the older houses has a chimney pot, only thought necessary for coal burning, and even then perhaps not afforded. Wood smoke was acceptable indoors.

Looking down White Street, Wallbrook, 1950s.

This quaint alley in Coseley was known officially as Bissell Street, but to local folk as 'The Duck Hole'. It presents an odd mixture of the older Wallbrook houses, and was demolished in the 1960s. It extended from the junction of Bridge Street and Angle Street, and reached Wallbrook Street.

The approach to Broad Street from Angle Street, 1950s. The footpath on the left goes to Railway Terrace (see book 2).

The car pauses at the exit from The Priory in Sedgley, about to enter the west end of Vicar Street, into Gospel End Street, or 'Bush Bank', autumn 1966. The Bush Inn stood on the site of the traffic island, centre of the picture, until about 1926.

Turl Street, Sedgley, 1970s. It has changed little, and remains an interesting example of the simple domestic architecture of times gone by.

May Street, Hurst Hill, August 1965. It was a quiet backwater linking the main thoroughfares of Clifton Street and Hollywell Street.

The Gullett, Cinderhill, 1965. These two- and three-storey properties were awaiting demolition. They present an interesting study in houses built above road level. Outhouses or workshops lie opposite.

A long view of Broad Street, Wallbrook, Coseley, 1950s. The street was densely populated and served by its own inns, shops and the Anglican Mission of St Cuthbert's. An esteemed pastor of the mission was Captain Budden (Church Army), who is now memorialised in a local road name.

Chapel Street, Wallbrook, 1950s. Its houses were built to suit the land contours. The new Council House building, at the bottom, will eventually replace them all.

Old houses in Hampton Street, Coseley, off Ivyhouse Lane, 1966. The new houses of Ward Street can be seen behind.

Jevon Street, Coseley, many houses already deserted and awaiting demolition, 1966. People would have sat on their front steps, taking the sun and sharing conversation.

The corner of Church Street and Humphrey Street, Lower Gornal, 1970s. The house has interesting ornamentation and hood moulded windows.

Dudley Street, Sedgley, reaches High Holborn, and Tipton Street slips away to the left to reach Tipton Road. Beyond the Primitive Methodist chapel on the left, and its graveyard, Turl Street turns to Turls Hill. The Grand Junction Inn is on the right.

Houses near the canal tunnel in Ivy House Lane, Coseley, 1960.

'The Big Fold' off Upper Ettingshall Road awaits demolition, 1960. It would have had a close community life all on its own.

# CHAPTER TWO

# FARMS & FARMING

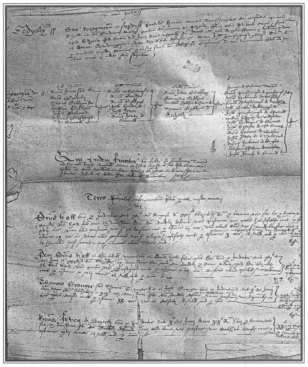

*One of Sedgley Manor's earliest known land
valuation documents: a page from the great Land Survey
of 1614. The first page contains names of jurors,
some of whose names are still found within the area –
Pensehouse, Jevons, Bradley, Gybbins, Whitehouse,
Cross, Hardwycke, Hickmans, Jukes, Follows, Hamons,
Button. Some of the field names mentioned can still be
located today.*

Remains of the wood bank to Himley Park can still be seen in the fields of Gospel End village, near Wood Farm and Gospel End Road. It would have been topped with a tall wooden palisade to retain the deer and to keep out the local population. The bank's distance from Himley gives an indication of the extent of the park.

Sandyfields Mill stood near the wood bank close to Sandyfields Road (west side), shortly after its junction with Cotwall End Road. The sketch, by Andrew Barnett, was taken from an original pencil drawing of Robert Noyes, of the famous Noyes family (Alfred was the author of 'Drake's Drum'). The original sketch was discovered by artist Ron Baker in a London showroom.

The old park of the castle was in the village of Woodsetton. This 1930s photograph shows its extensive lands and farmhouse long after it had been converted from lord's park to agriculture. It is now a Dudley housing estate, Old Park Farm.

These interesting cottages stood at the top of Ivyhouse Lane, just in old Ettingshall village. The photograph was taken in 1965, and the building has since been demolished. It had enjoyed an earlier agricultural history as a corn barn of the Caddick family.

A wooden store shed used by Mr L. Nicholls, whose family began farming at Red Lane in 1899. The family have possessed it for most of these years. Its age exceeds 100 years, as it was originally a shed at the Earl of Dudley's saw mills. It might have been purchased after the saw mills moved from the Level Site, Brierley Hill, in about 1850.

Hunt's mill and farm, Lower Gornal, 1930s. The water mill stands tall in the centre of the picture; this was an unusual mill as the wheel was inside the mill house. The farm and yard reveal the self sufficiency of the site. Best known locally as Hicken's Farm, it was demolished in the late 1970s.

Stables, outbuildings and carts behind a street in Gornal Wood, 1970s. It suggests that the time of dependence upon horses was not so long gone.

Derelict farm buildings at Ellowes Home Farm, 1960s.

Brownswall Farm, January 1962. Ron Baker's sketch (book 2) led to the discovery of the following photographs. The typical seventeenth-century stone construction was extended, and the dated medallion of 1720 refers only to the extension with room over the porch entrance. An entry in the 1614 Survey records a barn held by William Lawe in Sedgley. This first valuation could date the original house.

Brownswall Farm, seen from its entrance from Gospel End Road. Hamilton Close occupies the site today. For a while the farm's barn continued to encroach into two gardens on the northern side of Brownswall Road. The farmhouse was demolished in about 1964.

This view of the western aspect of the farmhouse shows the dovecote in the gable and the fine chimneys, while the high gables suggest that originally the roofs were thatched. A 1950s/'60s housing estate took its name from the farm, and occupies several of its fields.

Spout House Farm, Cotwall End, barley harvesting, 1970. Active farming continued here longer than in some similarly developing dormitory areas. Sadly Spout House Farm stands empty and neglected today, its fields bearing no crops. Its future will possibly be secured if it is converted into houses.

This view of cattle at Hunt's Mill, Lower Gornal, in the 1970s indicates how the mill house dominated the complex, as though emphasising its importance.

A winter view of Robert's Green Farm, Lower Gornal, seen from the north, 1979. Its outer garden walls are already showing signs of disrepair.

Nash's Farm, Gospel End, the first half of the twentieth century. This Price's postcard shows the farm's delightfully rural aspect, even though it was little more than a mile from the centre of Sedgley. A local wood went by the name of Nash's Coppice.

The potato harvest in 'Calves Croft' field, Spout House Farm, Cotwall End, October 1971.

Payne's Farm, Turls Hill Road. Turls Hill was in old Ettingshall. Remembered locally for its dairy produce, the farm has now been restored, and is named Charthouse Farm.

CHAPTER THREE

# HOUSES GREAT & SMALL

*A stone cottage in Parkes Lane, Woodsetton, 1959.*

Netherby Hall, Sedgley. The Victorian dream home of Major Haden declares visually that 'an Englishman's home is his castle'. This Price postcard reveals the Hall's elegance – with mews, and set in spacious grounds. The house was demolished in the 1960s, and today Caswell Road and Westridge occupy much of the site.

Turls Hill House approaching dereliction, September 1964. This ancient seat took on its stately home proportions after the occupancy of Ben Whitehouse, the ironmaster. It once housed Belgian refugees (see book 2), was sublet in sections and was finally demolished. The site still stands empty.

Roberts Cottage, Gospel End. Another Price postcard of the early twentieth century shows a rustic scene by including the cottage's splendid setting near Gospel End Common.

No. 9 Straits Green, Lower Gornal, March 1962. This stone cottage, with brick dormers, bore a date stone of 1680. It has been surrounded by the modern houses of the Straits.

Old lime kiln houses at Wrens Nest, Woodsetton, 1970. These cottages were built for the lime kiln tenders. Haphazard building often took place, sometimes with the Earl of Dudley looking the other way!

A view towards the lime kiln houses showing a disused quarry building and a recent bungalow, with its washing on a convenient open space. Modern housing developments lie in the valley beyond.

This stone house stood in High Street, Sedgley, opposite the entrance to Townsend Avenue. The brick gables are remarkably similar to those of the Straits Green house (page 43). It bears a date stone of 1680. The builder is unknown.

These stone houses were in Gordon's Place, Lower Gornal, not far from the Straits House. Unlike many of their neighbours these were built of the red sandstone that was readily accessible from a nearby quarry.

A Georgian house in Providence Row, Coseley, January 1962. Providence Row takes its name from the nearby Baptist church, whose first chapel was built here in 1783.

A stone cottage row off Ruiton Street, Lower Gornal, 1962. The stone between the right-hand dormers bore a date of 1715.

Capponfield House, Ettingshall, was built in 1842. The name was originally that of the area, Capon Field, but local usage decided otherwise. The land, between Broad Lanes and Highfields, once housed a significant ironworks (see page 95), and the house was once that of the works manager.

Crowesbridge House, Coppice Road, Upper Ettingshall, August 1965. The eighteenth-century house looks fit to be a home for many more years to come, but in five years it was gone. In 1999 a new housing estate occupied land behind the site, and took its name.

No. 66 Rookery Road, Vale Crest, Lanesfield, Ettingshall, home of the Porters, stands in extensive grounds between Rookery Road and the Birmingham New Road. The photograph was taken from fields across the road, before the post-war council houses were built.

This house in Clifton Street, Hurst Hill, revelled in a fine portico that was said to have graced the entrance of the first Wesleyan chapel in Can Lane (John Wesley was said to have preached under it). The old chapel was on the opposite side of the road to the present building. Seen here in 1963, the house was remembered as John Dunton's.

Coseley Hall, an engraving of 1850. The central section still stands. It was once the home of Richard Clayton, Manager of Cannon Iron Works. He was a benefactor in the area, giving the land for the Clayton Playing Fields.

These grand semi-detached houses on Tipton Road were the homes of the Parkes brothers, of Woodsetton Works (see books 1 and 2), makers of fire irons and fenders, and general ironware. An arched exit in their rear garden walls took them straight to the factory in Brook Street.

Woodsetton House, February 1962. It stood opposite the Rough Road, now a tarmac footpath (see page 11). The Mormon church now occupies the site. Woodsetton Lodge, House and Farm ran west to east along Tipton Road.

The Bayer Hall, Bayer Street, Coseley (see page 15). It became the main schools' clinic for Coseley, and a visit to Bayer Hall was most often remembered by schoolchildren as a visit to the dentist's.

Pitt's Cott, 1970s. This stood on the west side of Coseley Road, near to the border with Bilston. It was removed, brick by brick, and rebuilt at the Black Country Living Museum, Dudley.

The same cottage at a much earlier date, sporting half a tramcar as a conservatory. The left-hand window in the later view (above) had been a door. The railway truck behind bears the name Alfred Hickman, whose steelworks they served; the works became Stewarts and Lloyds in 1925.

A little single-storey cottage, John Street, Hurst Hill, November 1960. It makes an interesting contrast with the picture below.

Sedgley Park Hall. The Parkes family purchased the manor of Sedgley in 1600. In 1621 their surviving heiress was Frances Parkes, who married Humble Ward in 1628, bringing the Wards to the lordship of the manor. Their first home was at Sedgley Park. After the family's move to Himley, it became a Roman Catholic seminary, and finally the Park Hall hotel, which it remains. The imposing façade alone makes the house outstanding.

CHAPTER FOUR

# CHURCHES & CHAPELS

*The Roman Catholic mission church opened in
Sandyfields on St George's Day, 23 April 1789 (see
book 1), moving to its present site in 1823.
Occasionally coffin crosses have been recovered from
Sandyfields' gardens, as was this one – the gardens
once being the site of the burial ground.*

All Saints' Church, Sedgley, has a parish register dating from 1558. The second register, seen here, dates from 1685. Thomas Janns was vicar. The Persehouses (churchwardens) are a prominent local family. The beautiful script reminds us of an almost forgotten skill.

St Peter's Church, Upper Gornal, 1901. The foundation stone was laid by Lord Ward in 1838. Including the rebuilding of All Saints', it was the fifth church to be built during an Anglican expansion in the parish, encouraged by the Earls and overseen by the Revd Charles Girdlestone. The old National School is on the left.

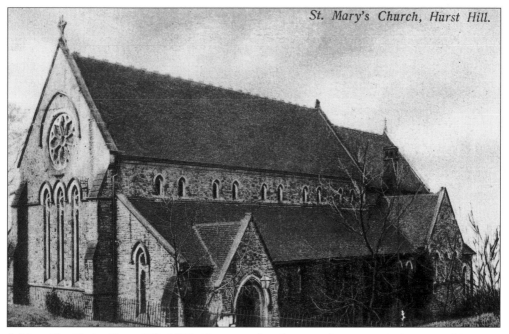

St Mary The Virgin, Hurst Hill, 1872. The stone church is seen here in an early twentieth-century Price's postcard. The church was built in Can Lane, on land given by H.B. Whitehouse, an ironmaster, and with a generous grant from the Earl of Dudley.

Christ Church, Coseley, was built as a 'chapel of ease' in 1830, and was later the parish church of Coseley. Reprocessing has restored this remarkable view of the church in 1868, seen from the vicarage garden. The vicar was the Revd Thomas Slater MA, who advertised in 1867 that he was 'distributing soup daily during the winter months'.

Seventeenth-century memorial plaque in All Saints' Church, Sedgley. Until the nineteenth century the church was the only parish church for this extensive area. The wood referred to is Gornal Wood.

St James The Great, Lower Gornal, dates from 1823, and was photographed in 1972. It was the earliest of the new Anglican chapels of ease in Sedgley, built so that the parishioners didn't have to travel so far to the parish church. St James' first vicar, the Revd Theodosius Theodosius, was a former minister of Ruiton Independent Chapel.

The vicarage of St James the Great, Lower Gornal, photographed here in 1970, after it had become vacant and prior to demolition.

The Old Meeting House, Coseley, 1982. The work really began after 1662, though this present building dates only from 1875 (see book 2).

Five Ways Methodist church, Lower Gornal, 1972. The chapel is thought to have been converted from a barn and cottages in 1841. Later the cottages were brought into use as classrooms. A new foyer now provides a covered access to the stairs for the upper rooms on the left.

Tipton Street Methodist church, Sedgley, 1974. The chapel moved from the small building still standing in Gospel End Street (see book 1) in 1857. Although listed, there is a threat of demolition. Its attractive Dutch gable and distinctive windows would be a loss from a charming and well-preserved streetscape along the north side of Tipton Street.

Mount Zion Methodist Church, Upper Gornal. The congregation leaves after a Sunday school anniversary service. This building was demolished in the 1970s when a new Upper Gornal Methodist church was built (see book 1).

Mount Zion's interior. The children sit upon their platform with an appropriate text on the wall behind them. The wooden anniversary platform, usually erected in time for the final rehearsal, remained in the church over the two Sundays of the festival.

Mount Zion's seventy-six singers of 1937 required an even higher platform, which was robustly constructed in bolted sections. Soon after the concluding service the platform was removed, and stored until the following year.

Upper Ettingshall Methodist church, 1970. A glimpse of Upper Ettingshall road, above Paul Street, on the left – with the shop and the Black Horse (see book 2) the first buildings in the row. A harsh eighteenth-century past gave the area the name Sodom, adopted affectionately now. The church is still known locally as Sodom chapel.

The marriage of Robert William James and Daisy Griffiths at Upper Ettingshall Methodist church, 25 June 1938. The blonde boy giving the horseshoe is Derek Garbett, while the dark-haired boy is Gerald Screen, both nephews of the bride.

St Barnabas, Church of England Mission at Gospel End, in a distinctly rural setting, captured on this Price's postcard in the early twentieth century. It is now a private residence.

St Aiden's Mission Church (1883) near the end of its life in 1970. This Mission church owed its allegiance to Christ Church, Coseley. It stood a little away from Hall Green Street, Bradley, facing resolutely towards its mother church. Chimneys at Highfields Works are seen on the left, and a glimpse of the Wesleyan chapel's tower on the right, behind the trees, in nearby Hall Green Street.

Holy Trinity, Ettingshall, Sunday school children, 1956. The reward for attendance at most Sunday schools wa
usually a book prize. Christmas parties and Sunday school outings were also arranged. Among those assembled fo

an outing are Lotty (née Lester) Kitson and daughter Lily, Judith and Dilys Morris, Gill Lester, Diane Smith, Christine Johnson and Colin Hyde.

Roseville Methodist church, Bayer Street, Coseley, 1912. This interior shot was prompted perhaps by the Harvest Festival. In true non-conformist style it has a high central pulpit to address ground floor and gallery, while its choir gallery and organ provide support from behind.

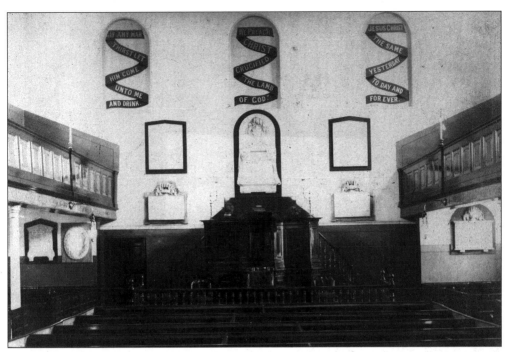

Darkhouse Baptist church interior, 1907. Again, a central pulpit underlines its importance, while a 'trinity' of texts gives emphasis to the Bible. This church was rebuilt in 1999, but retained part of the original external façade.

The second and final Ladymoor Methodist chapel, 1967. (The first chapel can be seen in book 1.) It was built in 1903 and stood on Broadlanes at the corner with Withy Lane; it was closed in 1976. Although the chapel was eventually demolished, the tree in its grounds still flourishes.

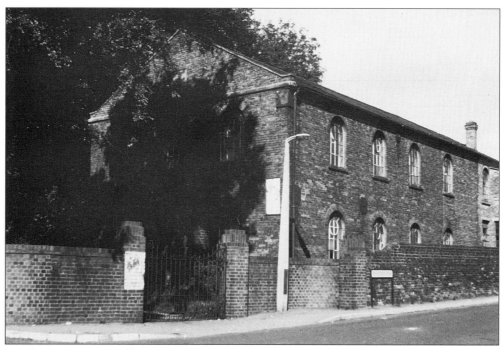

The 1809 building of Providence Baptist church. Coseley members from Darkhouse, living in West or 'Old' Coseley, began their own meetings, leading to this first church. It became the Sunday school after the building of a more ornate chapel in 1871 (see book 1).

The Revd Charles Girdlestone was a notable vicar of Sedgley, who appears in the *Dictionary of National Biography*. Here the bell that bore his name is removed for re-casting in 1975.

CHAPTER FIVE

# SHOPS & SERVICES

*Guest's butcher's shop, Hill Street, Ruiton, shortly*
*after closure in 1973. It was more properly known as*
*C.G. Guest and Son.*

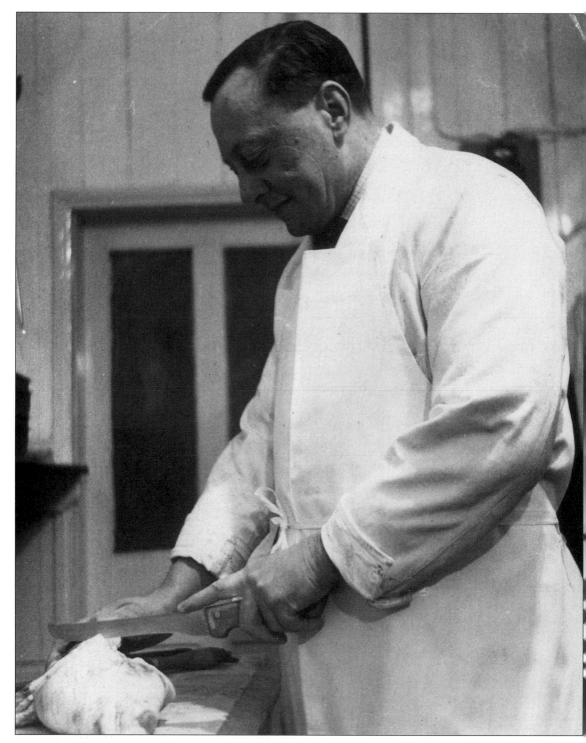

Alfred Guest at work in his shop (pictured on the previous page), shortly before closure. The business also provided door-to-door delivery. Mr Guest is also remembered for once being a fine left-handed batsman. After closure the premises were used by Dusty's (see book 1).

Spring House, shop and garage, Clarence Street, Upper Gornal, *c.* 1947. Edward (Ted) Pyatt stands in front. This is now the site of a large multiple garage.

Mrs Miriam Pyatt in front of the family's single-storey shop, 1940s. The array of advertisements is impressive; cream ices were part of the family's repertoire.

Behind Spring House was Spring Farm Dairy. This early milk hand-cart contrasts with the motorised fleet below.

The Pyatt family and workers pose before their impressive array of milk delivery vehicles, 1930s.

A well-remembered ironmonger's and hardware shop in Sedgley Bull Ring was White's. Here Mrs White and son Gilbert pose on the steps in 1929, with their wares arranged around them.

Huband's cake shop, 1970. It stood north of the Bull Ring, near to the Bilston Street junction. In the nineteenth century it had been the nail warehouse of John Elwell, whose descendants began the well-known Elwell tool firm, at Wednesbury.

This stone house stood at the bottom of Dean Street, Sedgley, and was photographed in winter 1970. Its ground floor was partly a dispensary for Egginton the Chemist (see book 1) and partly used by Repairwell cleaners.

Leonard Tranter's shop in Clifton Street, Hurst Hill, late 1920s. Mr and Mrs Tranter stand outside the shop, with baby Iris. Mr Tranter had lost an arm at Sankey's Manor Works.

W.H. (Bill) Fletcher had his cycle shop in Louise Street, Gornal Wood, for about forty years. Many Gornal boys and girls had their bikes from him. He kept a complete record of all bicycles sold, and their purchasers.

The mixture of old and new shops in the Bull Ring, 1968.

A derelict shop on the Sedgley side of Millfields Road, Ettingshall, 1957. Awaiting demolition, it had served the surrounding works in its later years. Much earlier it had been a 'tommy shop', where workers received part of their wages in goods.

# CHAPTER SIX

# PUBLIC HOUSES

*The Great Western Hotel, Daisy Bank (formerly Hall Fields),*
*1957. It still stands practically unchanged. However, the*
*Great Western Railway line, and Daisy Bank station, whose*
*passengers it once hoped to serve, went in Dr Beeching's plan!*

Hurst Hill Tavern, at the south end of Clifton Street, has had a facelift since this photograph was taken in 1957.

Even more changed is Coseley Tavern at the south end of Upper Ettingshall Road. This photograph dates from about 1900, and two bay windows have been added to the ground floor since that time.

The Rookery Tavern, Wood Street, Lanesfield, after the Second World War. The photograph shows the street sign still pointing to the public air-raid shelters! Landlord at the time was William Bayliss; previously it had been Stephen Rhodes.

This photograph provides a reminder of Hanson's Malt House on Gospel End Road. The new Seven Stars Inn now occupies the site.

The pub with two faces! Seen from Biddings Lane bridge, Coseley, in the 1970s, The Boat shows its older house, facing the canal it was built to serve. An archway in a wall and steps still provide access from the towpath.

Times change, and a second house was built, back to back, providing access for local people, road users and passengers from the old Deepfields LMS railway station. This view was taken in 1965.

The Summerhouse Inn, School Street, Coseley, 1960. This was another delicensed inn. The area has now been radically changed for the Green Street by-pass.

The White Horse, Upper Ettingshall Road, at the foot of Hurst Hill, undergoing renovations in 1961. This refit changed it to its present appearance.

The former Brickmaker's Arms, Broad Lanes, Ladymoor, 1960. It was often known locally as Shutty's, Mr Shutt being one of its landlords.

The Rifle Corps Inn, Clifton Street, Hurst Hill, 1960. It was already delicensed when this photograph was taken. It gave its name to Rifle Street, one of the old Hurst Hill streets between Clifton Street and Hollywell Street.

An illuminated address presented posthumously to a man of many parts. The family of Tom Griffiths, landlord of the Fountain Inn, Temple Street, Lower Gornal, were the recipients.

The Druid's Head, Caddick Street, in The Coppice, was demolished in the 1960s along with most of the accompanying houses (see book 2).

The Anchor Inn, Deepfields was another pub that served the canal before the locality. Anchor Lane led unerringly to it (see page 9).

The Forge Hammer, Spring Road, Lanesfield, 1977. The factories around it are already deserted. leaving no forge hammerers as customers. It used to be known in the local dialect as 'The Foj Ommer'.

The Crooked House is included for its special relationship with Lower Gornal. Traditionally frequented in the past by many of the miners working at the Himley coalfield, it stands across the boundary in old Himley parish. The same miners probably helped to undermine it. It is famous for its illusions, seen by the sober too – for example, marbles rolling up a table!

The Painter's Arms, Avenue Road, Coseley, *c.* 1965. It was an old inn, with sash cord windows and bay windows added later. The house is one of Holden's, the local brewers of Woodsetton.

The Queen's Arms in Hollywell Street, Hurst Hill, 1965. It was not long before the streets and pub were cleared and replaced with modern housing.

# CHAPTER SEVEN

# THE INDUSTRIAL PAST

*Sandstone grinding down the Holloway, Upper Gornal,
early twentieth century. Mr Charles Harper is on
the left.*

The site of the stone grinding looking west, early twentieth century. Ruiton's mill still has its sails and tail, though is already disused. The roofs are of houses in Vale Street.

Bagley's Quarry, Ruiton. Men pause for a photograph in the early twentieth century. The large blocks of sandstone can be seen behind. Shaping is taking place. We presume that the bowler hats denote seniority.

The damaged site of stone extraction. Large community dependence on the industry ensured that no environmental issues were considered. Quarries existed on both sides of Clarence Street, Upper Gornal, then the main road between Dudley and Wolverhampton. This quarry approaches the rear of Spring House (see page 71).

The site of stone grinding almost reaching Clarence Street, 1908. Upper Gornal Board School, later called Tudor, is across the road, while the older farmhouse near the edge is the Old Cottage of Content Inn. Jeavons's grocery shop is next to the school.

An old working 'gin' pit in Burton Road, Upper Gornal, still extracts coal in the 1920s. The horse, the gin, the colliers' 'boffy', the hand-propelled surface trucks and the deep rutted track in the foreground complete the scene.

A gin pit at Parkfield Colliery, early 1900s. It was considered worthy of a Price's postcard and had a general title to broaden sales. It was a common enough sight throughout the Black Country.

Ellowes Colliery Gin, still working in 1926. Collieries to the west were often in the countryside, to which it has returned, unless new housing has been built on the site.

Baggeridge Colliery, Gospel End, 1964. This deep mine yielded its first coal early in the twentieth century. Owned by the Earl of Dudley, it transformed the scale of local coal extraction and provided work for many Gornal folk, and beyond.

A school party from Redhall Junior School visits Baggeridge Colliery, 1964. Westwood's lorry, from Castle Street, Sedgley, is being loaded for domestic delivery.

A historic remnant of Capponfield Iron Works, Ettingshall, 1960s. This section of the furnace wall is being reclaimed by nature.

Alfred Hickman's iron and steel works, seen here when it was Stewarts and Lloyds, straddled the Ettingshall/Sedgley boundary with Bilston. It provided work for both communities, and many Sedgley steel workers entered the works over the Tenscore canal bridge.

The foreground shows the furnace waste (clinker) of the old Coseley Furnaces, 1970s. The houses and gardens are on the south side of Ladymoor Road, and beyond can be seen the wastes and buildings of British Steel, Spring Vale.

The firebrick works of W.R. Mobberley, 1964. There were two brickworks on the site originally, between Hurst Road and Upper Ettingshall Road, the Victoria and Breen Rhydding.

This evidence of a domestic hearth remained for many years. Here a brick workshop can be seen in Hill Street, Ruton, next to a stone house.

This metal pressings die yard was cleared in 1999. It belonged to John Thompson Motor Pressings, founded in 1904. Most of the dies dated from when cars were built on strong metal chassis. Among the white-painted marks on the dies was R.R. for Rolls-Royce.

In 1964 the Loxdale Engineering Company stood on the west side of Spring Road, Lanesfield. It was a part of the John (Jackie) Norton group.

The Safe Works, Dudley Road, Upper Gornal, May 1963. A number of safe makers worked in the area from the nineteenth century onwards. Most well known was Stephen Cox & Son of Dudley Road. Some of their safes are still in use today.

Gough's was a brass foundry working in the heart of Wallbrook, Coseley. Making brass ornaments and novelties was one of their specialities. 'Guff's', as it was often known, stood between White Street, Bissell Street and Chapel Street.

Samuel Brookes began trading in Gospel End Street, Sedgley, in 1904, when works were developing on a large scale. The family company continued through sons and grandsons. Their skills were used for various products and here we see advertised a range of Sedgley woodworker's tools.

Alice Millard, one of five family relatives who worked for the firm, operates a pillar drill in the Brookes factory.

Brookes grandchildren enjoy a sunny break outside the works, late 1950s. With them, third from the left, is the well-known Sedgley electrician the late Roger Fellows, who with his brother John had an electrical shop in Bilston Street. The family are, left to right, Graham, Janet and Alan.

More evidence of the manor's old cottage industries can be seen in these back-yard buildings, behind Bridge Street and White Street, Coseley. These resemble nail shops.

The vast hole created by clay extraction at Woodsetton, 1960s. Years of spasmodic infilling took place before the hole was filled. Now new houses stand on the site.

This marl hole, seen here in 1966, created problems in Lower Gornal when it filled with water. It was the cause of several swimming fatalities.

Barn-like outhouses behind Summer House Row, Hurst Hill, 1960s (see page 124).

Round Hill Limestone Quarry, Sedgley Beacon, seen here returning to nature in the 1970s, was known to be working in 1680. It has now been designated a Site of Special Scientific Interest.

# CHAPTER EIGHT

# SCHOOLS

*Old Hurst Hill School's playground, August 1965. To the right is the traditional toilet block, across the yard!*

Another view of the school (also known as St Mary's), showing a classroom next to the playground – and showing how compact the site was.

Sedgley's National School, off Vicar Street, was a gift of John William Earl of Dudley in 1828. It was known also as the Charity School, or the Sunday School, which it was before the new parish hall was built. Here in 1970 demolition had begun, and the site was for sale. Today a supermarket, shops and a car park are here.

Red Hall Girls School staff, Gornal Wood, 1932. Standing, left to right: Misses Kytes, Powell, Mark, Braddock and Bradford. Seated: Miss J. Hale, Mrs Harvey, Misses Bolger, Allen and E. Smith. Anyone attending school before the Second World War will recall a similar room. One of the pictures on the wall will be of King George V and Queen Mary.

Lanesfield Council School, Wood Street, Lanesfield, 1934. Back row, left to right: -?-, Tommy Clarke, Eric Waterhouse, Bert Jeavons, Jack Hewitt, Leslie Large, Fred Watson. Third row: May Bennett, Vera Boulton, Dorothy Clarke, Kathy Jeavons, Doreen Shaw, Dorothy Clempson, Joan Clarke, Mary Felton, Ivy Young, Sylvia Genge, Dorothy Richards, Joyce Dell. Second row: Annie Churms, ? Hardwick, Cathy Dawes, Alice Fullard, Annie Ball, Kathleen Harriman, Blanche Shinton, Dorothy Nann, Kathleen Hadley, Hilda Davis. Front row: Ernie Briscoe, Val Thomas, Doug Rhodes, -?-, ? Ford, Ron Croydon, Victor Fellows.

Lanesfield Council School, May Queen Festival, 1939. The May Queen was Joan Law. Her attendants, standing behind her, are Beryl Colley, the previous year's Queen (left), and Sheila Morris, who became Queen the following year (right).

The little school of St Chad's, Portland Place, West Coseley. A well-remembered headmistress was Miss E. Turner.

Queen Victoria School, Sedgley, the top class of 1940. Back row, left to right: Jack Roberts, Raymond Stephenson, Derek Bridgewood, Lionel Hickman, Roger Wallet, Billy Knight, Gordon Griffiths, Frank Slater, Raymond Harley. Fourth row: Christine Robson, June Southall, Joyce Wasdell, Dorothy Pugh, Beryl Gadd, Moire Hancox, Betty Gregory, Betty Hampton, Audrey Preston, Alice Siers. Third row: Betty Timmins, Betty Nicholls, Beryl Preston, Tess Griffiths, Beryl Jones, Hazel Southall, Doreen Vince, Christine Cotton, Pat Cooper. Second row: Keith Robbins, John Flavell, Joan Price, Irene Dunn, Iris Harley, Rita Stanley, Olive Smith, Francis Lloyd, Billy Slater, Jack Jones. Front row: Raymond Barnett, Leonard Haden, Jeffry Webb, Ken Williams, Harry Roderick, Jack Shinton, Fred Nicholls, Sidney Southall, Leslie Baker. The headmaster, standing on the left, is Mr McLeod and the class teacher on the right is Mr Hughes.

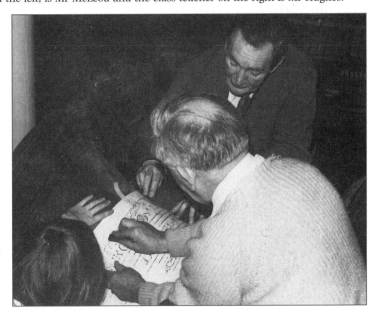

Headmasters W.R. (Ray) Gowland (facing) and F.A. (Andrew) Barnett of Bramford and Red Hall Primary Schools respectively prove that 'two heads are better than one' as they demonstrate brass rubbing to pupils copying the inscriptions on All Saints' bells, 1975.

Sedgley and Upper Gornal Board Schools children gather at Upper Gornal School (later Tudor School) for Empire Day celebrations, 24 May 1934. Back row, left to right: Irene Bennett. Alice Price, Emmie Porter, Ellen Bruce, Annie Cartwright, Vera Mustoe, Ethel Clark, Doris Porter, Muriel Walker, Joan Pyatt, Irene Abbiss. Third row: Phyllis Raybould, Helen Carter, Elsie Harley, Nellie Nicholls, Vera Naylor, Mary Harper, Lily Williams, Kathy Sheldon, Mary Bennett, Joan Cooper. Second row: Kathy Taylor, Mary Bate, Jane Brittle, Irene Dutton, Dolly Edwards, Mavis Bodenham, Peggy Mustoe, May Cartwright, Gerty Cowdell, Matilda Westwood. Front row: Bessie Marsh, May Nicholls, Betty Wright, Mary Bradley, Amy Darby, Doris Darby.

One of Coseley's most influential headmasters, Leonard Jackson, stands outside his school at Broad Lanes.

# CHAPTER NINE

# LIFE & TIMES

*Violet Turton, Chairman of Coseley Council, and on the right Clerk of the
Council Joseph Roper, 1955/56.*

Sedgley Urban District Council pose for a final photograph before Urban District status was removed in April 1966. Left to right: William Shield, Fred Phipps, George Beswick, Lawrence Jeavons, David Gregory, Harold Smith, Stan Dews, Ken Newton (clerk), Joe Jones, Tom Hanley, Albert Turner (chairman), -?- (behind), Albert Oakley, Jack Pugh, Michael Kinsella, Tom Parkin, Jim Fithern, Alan Hickling, Bruce Meredith, -?-, Les Pugh.

Sedgley police gather outside the police station, late 1920s. The sergeant on the left of the front row is Thomas Hall. On the noticeboard is an early recruiting poster for the RAF.

The foundation stone for the Green Street Council House shows those who served in 1895. Richard Clayton, of Coseley Hall, was chairman that year.

Coseley Council meeting, 1962. Standing, left to right: S. Nicholls, Les Adams, Stan Cox, Dr Joseph Needoff, Sam Martin, Helen Beach, George Beach. Seated: Cllrs John (Jack) Pointon, Bill Perkins (chairman) Joseph W. Roper (clerk), Ernest Childs JP, Frank Wagstaff, Allen Hackford, Cyril Oliver, Tom Fieldhouse, Mary Pointon, Violet Turton, Jack Wilson, Harry Poole. Florence Richards and Clarence Parkes were not present.

Coseley police station, Avenue Road, in the process of demolition, 1967.

Coseley fire station, School Street, with hose-drying tower, 1960s.

A gathering by the summer house at a vicarage garden party held at All Saints' Church, Sedgley, at about the time of the First World War.

A gathering of the local Civil Defence and First Aiders during the Second World War. The photograph was taken in the garden of Howell's Paddock, Upper Gornal. Among those present are Joyce and Annie Bealle, Alice Westwood, Fred Porter and Marion Fownes (later Mrs Porter), ? Fellows, and Mr Aston, Dudley registrar. The grounds were used for many local events, and sometimes a band played on the terrace behind.

*Best wishes*

*Trevor Genge*

*30 - 10 - 99*

*cyril JAy!*

~~Harry~~ Jevon and his sister Dorothy were a well-known Sedgley couple who ran a dancing school, which was especially popular during the Second World War. 'Old Time' was particularly popular, as the New Year's Ball ticket shows, and the advert on the back for their weekly classes. The prices would make them popular today!

After the Second World War several efforts were made to provide better facilities for senior citizens. Here is Sedgley Pensioners' Club shortly after its opening.

An early committee of the Pensioners' Club. At the centre stands the chairwoman, well-known and hard-working local councillor Mrs E. Williams.

The height of the pensioners' year was the annual holiday to the seaside.

Possibly behind the Britannia Inn, Upper Gornal, 1920s. The charabanc waits to take an outing of the Grand Order of Buffalos, Beacon Lodge (The Buffs), whose headquarters were at the inn. John Marson is second from left.

A crowd of children gather to watch a pig roast in the Red Lion yard, 1930s. The bunting is hanging in Mill Bank, perhaps for the Coronation?

The popular local sport of pigeon flying is less evident today. Here in 1965 this garden loft in Holywell Street, Hurst Hill, was one of many to be seen around the district.

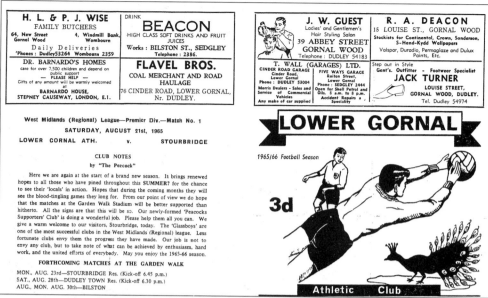

West Midlands (Regional) League—Premier Div.—Match No. 1
SATURDAY, AUGUST 21st, 1965
LOWER GORNAL ATH.  v.  STOURBRIDGE

### CLUB NOTES
by "The Peacock"

Here we are again at the start of a brand new season. It brings renewed hopes to all those who have pined throughout this SUMMER? for the chance to see their 'locals' in action. Hopes that during the coming months they will see the blood-tingling games they long for. From our point of view we do hope that the matches at the Garden Walk Stadium will be better supported than hitherto. All the signs are that this will be so. Our newly-formed 'Peacocks Supporters' Club' is doing a wonderful job. Please help them all you can. We give a warm welcome to our visitors, Stourbridge, today. The 'Glassboys' are one of the most successful clubs in the West Midlands (Regional) league. Less fortunate clubs envy them the progress they have made. Our job is not to envy any club, but to take note of what can be achieved by enthusiasm, hard work, and the united efforts of everybody. May you enjoy the 1965-66 season.

FORTHCOMING MATCHES AT THE GARDEN WALK

MON., AUG. 23rd—STOURBRIDGE Res. (Kick-off 6.45 p.m.)
SAT., AUG. 28th—DUDLEY TOWN Res. (Kick-off 6.30 p.m.)
AUG., MON. AUG. 30th—BILSTON

**LOWER GORNAL**
1965/66 Football Season
**3d**
Athletic   Club

Of all the local football teams, Lower Gornal's, at the Garden Walk Stadium, led the way. Here in this 1965 programme was a team that included two players who later achieved senior league status. The programme also provides a wealth of information about local advertisers, many of them now gone.

This NALGO Ball appears to have taken place in the Manor School Hall, Ettingshall Road, late 1930s.

This Brookes Engineering truck (see pages 97 and 98) is being used to take the All Saints' Church Young Men's Group on an outing in 1929. Left to right: Tom Cochrane, Jack Beddard, Leslie Jennings, Rupert Turner, Harry Flavell, Harry Allden and Reg Allden. No concern seems to have been expressed about the driver!

A Coseley carnival float preparing to move off from Bayer Street, *c*. 1930. The float represents the Alexandra Rose charity, founded by Queen Alexandra in 1912 to help fund hospitals. The children's floral costumes were made from pink crêpe paper. Only one child can be identified, Hilda Jeavons, nearest the cab in the middle row.

WHO PUT THE PIG ON THE WALL AT GORNAL TO SEE THE BAND GO BY.

WAS IT.

BILLY THE BOY.
JIMMY THE GO.
CLOCKWEIGHT.
BILLY ON THO'B.
THE POKEY MON.

OR

JACKO.
TASSO.
COGGER.
BLOSSOM.
JACKERY.

?

The story of Gornal's pig on the wall is now preserved in an Upper Gornal pub name. That a pig was put on the wall to watch a band go by is more than likely, so popular was the local pig, The back-yard sty continued to be commonplace until after the Second World War. The card shown is likely to have been adapted from one circulating in the village of Dawley to welcome the Channel swimmer Captain Webb.

## CHAPTER TEN
# ASPECTS & PROSPECTS

*Stone cottages were a feature of The Gornals. These were demolished in the 1970s.*

This view of Sedgley village is taken from the west, where Ettymore Estate now stands. The 'new' graveyard seems to have plenty of land, and the whole scene might appear to show a rural community.

The deep cleft of the canal cutting at Coseley seems hardly reclaimed by nature in this view from School Street bridge. The broken landscape and distant industry is evident.

A view of Sedgley Bull Ring from All Saints' Church roof, 1970. The old water tanks still stand by the Beacon Tower.

The Beacon Tower. This Price's postcard has been taken from a particularly favourable angle and reinforces the rural aspects much cherished locally.

Sedgley Bull Ring activity, 1900. Work is taking place for the change to electric trams. We mustn't miss the other signs of older times, such as the water cart, standing by the central lamppost, or the awning of Carmi Fox's butcher's shop. The Clifton now occupies that corner.

Gospel End Common was as pleasant as this 1920s Price's postcard depicts it: it was a popular 'lung' within easy walking distance.

Another romantic rural postcard scene, described as being in Whites Lane, perhaps indicates the growing longing for a lost heritage. Whites Lane joins Turls Hill to the Beacon ridge path at Bilston Street.

A Hurst Hill view looking east towards Barr Beacon shows the familiar scene of clustered chimneys descending the hill, while in the foreground, on the left, is the rear of a 'local', the Miner's Arms.

A derelict building in Hurst Hill, 1967. Known by a couple of names, the institute and the pawn shop (it was used as both), it stood near the end of Walter Street, or Summer House Row, on what locals call 'Johnny Cornfield's backside'.

Sedgley Bull Ring, east side, 1968. Many changes have occurred even in this familiar view – including the Red Lion yard and its frontage, and the ownership of businesses.

This photograph from Hermits Row/Rock Street, Upper Gornal, shows the new housing of Cricket Meadow and Robert Street, with Roberts Green Farm and Gibbons Works prominent features. The three tower blocks at Eve Hill, Dudley, instantly recognisable from miles away, were reduced to one on 18 July 1999.

# ACKNOWLEDGEMENTS

The author acknowledges his gratitude to many people and sources of both pictures and information used in this book. Every effort has been made to contact all copyright holders of photographs.

I thank the *Wolverhampton Express and Star*, the *Birmingham Post and Mail*, Dudley Archives and Local History Service, Wolverhampton Archives and Local History Service, the Black Country Society, Sedgley Museum and Lanesfield Primary School.

I have been helped considerably by the collections of Mrs Margaret Roper, and her late husband John, and by Mrs Roper's advice. The work has been further enhanced by the collection of the late John Grainger, that of the late F. Andrew Barnett, the late Richard Dews and Mrs E. Groucutt. Once more I have been supported throughout by the indefatigable Ron Baker.

Acknowledgement is also made to Eddie Attwood, Denys Baker, Gill Bates, Beryl Bayliss, Joyce Beale, Alan and Ann Brookes, Doris Cole, Ron Davies, Stan Dews, Irene Dicken, the late J.T. Egginton, Sylvia Genge, Joe and Mary Harper, Anne Hartland, Carl Higgs, Jenny Hill, Bryan Hollies, Marion Hyde, Robert James, Frank and Kitty Jones, Jack Jones, Jack Moore, Lawrence and Mary Nicholls, John Pearson, Pat Porter, Sue Powell, Neville Price, Gerald Screen, Hilda Stanford, Gilbert White, Janet Williams and Mr S.A. Williams. The staff of COLAB Wolverhampton have offered valuable technical advice together with their usual efficient and cheerful service.